Songs of Praise based on the Bhagavad Gita

Saroj Daulat Ram

Published by:

2011/2017

Songs of Praise based on the Bhagavad Gita

by **Saroj Daulat Ram**

Published by:
In Our Words, Inc.
inourwords.ca

Cover design:
Anindita Modak

Library and Archives Canada Cataloguing in Publication

Ram, Saroj Daulat
Songs of parise based on the Bhagavad Gita / Saroj Daulat Ram
Poems.

ISBN   978-1-926926-10-0

1. Bhagavadgita--Poetry. 1. Title.

P S8635. A461S66 2011   C2011-906741-2

First Printing, October 2011
Reprint, September 2017

All Rights Reserved. © estate of Saroj Daulat Ram, 2011/2017. No part of this book may be reproduced in whole or in part, in any form, or stored on any device including digital media, except with the prior written permission of the publisher. Exceptions are granted for brief quotations utilized in critical articles or reviews with due credit given to the author.

Dedication

To my grandchildren
Anand, Anjali, Sonia,
Monica, Anand,
Kashia & Sachin
and to
children everywhere

O Supreme Lord!
Vasu deva sutum devam
Kamsa-can ura-mardanam
Devaki perma nandam
Krishnam vande jagadgurum

O Divine son of Vasu Deva,
slayer of the tyrant council,
Devaki's supreme joy,
I salute thee Krishna,
Lord of the Universe!

Contents

PREFACE

CHAPTER 1
Arjuna's Sorrow 3

CHAPTER 2
The Book of Doctrines 4

CHAPTER 3
Virtue in Work 6

CHAPTER 4
Religion of Knowledge 8

CHAPTER 5
Karma-Sanyas Yoga 10

CHAPTER 6
Religion of Self-Restraint 11

CHAPTER 7
Vijnana Yoga Religion by Discernment 13

CHAPTER 8
Akshara Parabrahma Yoga 15

CHAPTER 9
Supreme Knowledge and Mystery 16

CHAPTER 10
Book of Heavenly Perfections 18

CHAPTER 11
Manifesting the One & Manifold 20

CHAPTER 12
Bhakti Yoga - Religion of Faith 23

CHAPTER 13
Separation of Matter from Spirit 25

CHAPTER 14
Gunatrayavibhaga Yoga 27

CHAPTER 15
Religion by Attaining the Supreme 29

CHAPTER 16
Separation of the Divine from the Secular 30

CHAPTER 17
Threefold Kinds of Faith 31

CHAPTER 18
Yoga of Renunciation and Deliverance 33

POSTSCRIPT
IN THE FINAL ANALYSIS
OHM
ABOUT THE AUTHOR

Preface
The Bhagavad Gita (Lord's Song)

The Bhagavad Gita is the most important text of Hinduism, written over twenty centuries ago as a centerpiece of the great epic of Mahabharata, in which the royal cousins, Kurus and Pandus fight for the Kingdom of Bharat (ancient name of India). The Kurus had usurped the kingdom from the Pandus in a crooked game of dice, which led to a war between the heirs of the royal house on the field of Kurukeshtra (located near present day New Delhi).

  Prince Arjuna, a stalwart warrior and one of the five Pandu brothers, is helped by Lord Krishna, his cousin and charioteer, who is also the Avatar (embodiment) of Lord Vishnu. Lord Krishna has come to earth to let good triumph over evil. When Prince Arjuna faces his cousins, uncles, teachers, and relatives whom he may have to destroy in battle, he becomes acutely distressed, lays down his weapons and refuses to shed the blood of his revered elders in the impending battle.

Thereupon, Lord Krishna, his charioteer, explains to him the meaning of good against evil, of doing one's rightful duty (dharma), and of treading the path of righteousness. Arjuna is convinced that salvation lies in doing one's duty to the best of one's ability.

Sanjay is the narrator of the story to the blind King Dhiritrashtra, who is the Kuru king. The story is told in 18 chapters, consists of over 700 couplets and is composed in Sanskrit by the sage Vyasa. The Bhagavad Gita immortalizes the epic Mahabharata and is read daily by millions of people all over the world. It is a treatise on the yoga of action; since we are given a life to live, how should we face it and live it?

That is the message of the Bhagavad Gita.

Saroj Daulat Ram
Georgetown, 2011

Chapter 1
Arjuna's Sorrow

Dhiritrashtra, the blind king of the Kurus asks Sanjay his messenger: "How goes the battle between the Kurus and Pandavs on the field of Kurukeshtra, on the field of Dharamkeshtra (righteousness)?"

SANJAY: Prince Arjuna on surveying the battlefield is filled with distress, loses his desire to fight when he sees that the enemies are in fact his cousins, uncles, brothers, teachers, sages and seers, whom he once held so dear, and whom he might have to slay. This is what happened:

ARJUNA to KRISHNA, his charioteer:
In pity lost, plagued by doubts, I shall not slay my kinfolk and friends in battle this day. It is better to live on beggar's bread with those we love alive than to slay one's kinfolk and guiltily survive. No victory won with such blood can give delight, even if my lost kingdom is their prize.

Chapter 2
The Book of Doctrines

Sanjay continues the story:
On seeing Arjuna so despondent, Lord Krishna gives the following advice:

KRISHNA: The soul is indestructible, Arjuna, and the Spirit within it never dies. At death it merely casts away the body and is reborn in a new body; cast away this cowardly fit, Arjuna. It is unbecoming of a warrior (a kashatrya). Do your dharma (duty) and destroy evil. Live in action, fight a righteous battle, not for the reward that comes from it, but for the sake of doing your duty.

ARJUNA: O Lord, what is the mark of a person with steadfast heart, who follows the path of yoga of action and meditation?

KRISHNA: If one ponders on the objects of the sense, there grows attraction and desire, which leads to passion and recklessness and ruin. Therefore, control your senses and lusts, meditate on God, live in dutiful action, do your duty, live by your righteous Dharma and not for the reward that comes from fighting the Good Fight. To destroy evil brought upon the kingdom by your kin is your duty. Shake off the yoke of flesh (cowardice), be a Karmayogi (doer of good deeds) so shall you reach Brahma, your Nirvana.

Live in action, fight a righteous battle,
not for the reward that comes from it,
but for the sake of doing your duty.

Chapter 3
Virtue in Work

ARJUNA: O Lord, if meditation is better than action, why do you impel me to fight this battle? Tell me truly—by what path will I find my ideal life—my salvation (Moksha)?

KRISHNA: There are two schools of thought, Arjuna. One is through meditation and spirituality and the other is through Yoga of Action, in which you do good deeds in order to bring deliverance to the world. In life you cannot stay idle. One must do good deeds unselfishly in order to keep the wheels of this world running for the better, and in so doing destroy evil. In performance of basic duty, we ascend to our highest bliss.

ARJUNA: O Lord, by what force is one drawn to evil ways?

KRISHNA: Passion (kama) pushes one to dark deeds. Passion deems fair but it is deceitful, and lures the mind to dark realms where one falters easily and goes to doom. Therefore, Arjuna, govern thy heart, resist sinfulness and that which saps the mind and judgement.

Higher than the flesh is the Mind, the Soul is higher still and God is higher than the Soul. Therefore, with God's help fight this battle in order to vanquish evil. O Prince of India, rise and fight the noble fight.

*In performance of basic duty,
we ascend to our highest bliss.*

Chapter 4
Religion of Knowledge

ARJUNA: O Lord Divine, reveal to me the history of thy many Avatars (Reincarnations), and the meaning of the Yoga (wisdom) passed down from age to age.

KRISHNA: From the beginning of time, this yoga was taught by me to many of the great saints such as Vaivasvata Manu, Ikshvaku, Vishnu and others. These were my different incarnations. When wickedness is strong and morality declines, I rise from age to age, taking a visible form, destroying evil, encouraging good, and reinstating virtue. Those who live a pious life, them will I exalt.

I created the four castes and portioned them according to human qualities. Those who do holy works without expecting reward are saintly and have mastered their sense of life, seeking truth, meditating on Brahma, sacrificing a life of pleasure, finding joy in worship at the altar flame. They reach me, the sacrifice that knowledge pays is better than great gifts of wealth. Seek the truth and bond with it. It shall carry you across your faults. Rise to your duty, cut the bond of ignorance and doubt, and be brave and wise. Trust in me and arise and take to the field of battle!

*Those who do holy works without
expecting reward are saintly and
have mastered their sense of life,
seeking truth, meditating on Brahma,
sacrificing a life of pleasure,
finding joy in worship at the altar flame.*

Chapter 5
Karma-Sanyas Yoga

(Renouncing Reward of Holy Work)

ARJUNA: O Lord, reveal to me that which is better of the two: Renunciation of all work and desires, or yoga of service through holy works?

KRISHNA: Better than surrender of all work is the service through holy work. Better still is the surrender of reward for thy selfless service in the name of God. Only then you shall find peace, and Nirvana you shall reach.

Surrendering all desires of the sensory world, find salvation in serving one supreme God.

Be a yogayukt – one who serves humanity.
Be equable in pleasure and pain, loss or gain.
Set your heart on Brahma.
Master your lust and passion.
Meditate on Brahma, so shall you find Nirvana.

Chapter 6
Religion of Self-Restraint

KRISHNA: A 'sanyasi' is a person who does holy works without expecting any reward for it. A true Renouncer is the one who worships through work, unmoved by passions of gain or loss, finding faith through unselfish service in the name of God.

ARJUNA: Lord, passions are difficult to control. They are wayward like the wind, tumultuous and impetuous.

KRISHNA: Prayerful meditation leads to self-restraint. This helps to curb passions and sense life.

ARJUNA: O Lord – what if one fails in self-restraint?

KRISHNA: No heart that holds even one right desire ever fails. Keep striving with full faith, sin-free, and self-purification leads to self-mastery. Practice Yoga. Be a Brahmacharya, lust-free, musing devoutly on the Lord you shall find peace of Nirvana. True piety removes earthly aches and troubles. Steadfastly practice self-control till it becomes effortless. Let your soul be ruled by the Supreme Soul. In such a state, we can see God in all living things.

ARJUNA: O Lord – the heart of man is unfixed, if he fails in his striving, is he not lost forever then?

KRISHNA: Those who strive are not lost. At death they come to the realm of the just, through many reincarnations they achieve perfection and then are not reborn. Be a yogi Arjuna, and dwell on the Supreme mystery of God with all your heart and soul.

---

*True piety removes
earthly aches and troubles.*

Chapter 7
Vijnana Yoga Religion by Discernment

KRISHNA: O Arjuna, know Me as I am, the very truth. I am Omnipresent in all my Creation and I am the Right Desire in all who yearn to know and to reach me.
Only four kinds of mortals know me –
>The one who weeps,
>the one who yearns to know,
>the one who toils to help, and
>the one who seeks to reach the Divine.

This last one is the highest.
Among votaries, this person is the best.
By trying to reach the Supreme,
one realizes the higher self, the Atman.
O Arjuna, know me as Adhiatman – the Soul of Souls.
>Adhibuta – as Lord of Life
>Adhideva – Lord of all Gods
>Adhiyajna – Lord of Sacrifice, this is the highest Form!

I am the Brahma, Soul of Souls, the very Truth. Seek refuge in Me. By so doing, you will be freed from the cycle of birth and death.

Hence worship Me with hearts of love and perfect faith and hold Me dear till the time of death, so shall you reach Me.

I am the Brahma, Soul of Souls, the very Truth.
Seek refuge in Me. By so doing,
you will be freed from
the cycle of birth and death.

Chapter 8
Akshara Parabrahma Yoga

(Devotion to One Supreme God)

ARJUNA: O Lord of lords – what is the Supreme Spirit and one's spiritual nature? What is Matter, Divinity and the Law? Who rules the Spirit of Sacrifice in man? At the time of death, how does a devotee find Thee and reach Thee?

KRISHNA: Brahma is the one Eternal God. Atman is His Spirit in each person. Karma is the force of Creation of life. Divinity inspires the spirit of sacrifice. Meditate with devotional faith in God.

Yoga of austere life will lead to the Lord. God is Unmanifest, Utmost, Infinite. All those who tread the highest path reach Brahma. They return no more to the earthly life of pain and suffering. These Karma yogis find eternal peace in a state of Nirvana.

Chapter 9
Supreme Knowledge and Mystery

KRISHNA: O Arjuna, hear now about my secret Mystery. I am the One Eternal God. I am the Soul of souls. Creating all, sustaining all, yet dwelling outside of it all, I create and destroy galaxies. I am the Eternal Source of Life, the Beginning and the End.

O Arjuna, I am the Sacrifice and the Prayer – the Mantra 'OHM.' I am the parent, the guardian of all creation, the wisdom of the four Vedas. I am the eternal Truth of all visible and invisible life. I am the Receiver and the Lord of every sacrifice. Those who follow lower gods, go to these at the time of death.

To be freed from the Karmabandu, worship the Divine Lord and none can perish who follow the righteous path in my name. Beings of all four castes, the Sudras, Vashyias, Kashtriyas,

Brahmans, all find Me if they make worshipful sacrifices in my name.

Hence Arjuna, thou Prince of India, fix your heart and mind on Me, serve Me, embrace your faith and reverence in Me, and thus your spirit shall be guided to the highest God and to your salvation at the time of death.

*To be freed from the Karmabandu,
worship the Divine Lord and none can perish
who follow the righteous path in my name.*

Chapter 10
Book of Heavenly Perfections

ARJUNA: O Lord, thou art Parbrahma, the Supreme Creator. In what manifestation will I know Thee and recognize Thee? By thy favour, reveal to me the secret of Thy Might and Majesty as the source of all Existence, so I may learn the wisdom of Thy manifestations here on Earth and in the Universe.

KRISHNA: O Arjuna, Kuru prince, I am the Spirit that dwells in the heart of all beings. I am the Evolution and its Creator, the sacred Ohm, I am. Sama Ved I am, the sun and the moon, I am endless life and boundless love. I am Gayatri Mantra, I am the splendour of the splendid, victory of a battle I am, of Pandus I am thou, of saints. I am Vyasa. I am the great unbroken silence in learning secret things. I am the Source of all and its Sustainer of life. I am the beginning, middle, and the end. I am the Self, as Soul, seated in mankind's heart, Giver of Divine vision to those pure of heart. Wisdom, talents and splendour come from me. I am the Silence of the hidden Mysteries. I pervade and sustain the Universe and am Creator of all things great and small. Know that I am, the Brahma, the Maker and the Destroyer of the Universe.

I pervade and sustain the universe
and am Creator of all things great and small.
Know that I am, the Brahma,
the Maker and the Destroyer of the Universe.

Chapter 11
Manifesting the One & Manifold

ARJUNA: O Lord, by thy favour reveal to me the splendour of Thy own Supreme Being. By Thy favour I have heard Thy spoken Word of Truth, of Soul and Spirit, of Karma and Dharma and yogis. Now I long to see the play of Thy Mystery with my mortal eyes, show me Thy very Self, as the Eternal God in Action.

KRISHNA: With mortal eyes thou cannot behold the Mystery Supreme in Action. I give thee Divine Sense and Sight, now behold my many forms as Creator and Destroyer.

Arjuna then beheld the manifold forms of the Lord, dazzling like a thousand suns, now creating, now destroying, galaxies forming and then disappearing. Countless mystic forms unfolding. Dazzled and amazed, Arjuna knelt and bowed his head and prayed thus:

ARJUNA: I see, Lord, all is encompassed in Thee as all creatures in Thee dwell. Then I see Thee as Brahma seated on His lotus throne as Lord of all Eternity, with brilliance blazing, the planets quake with Thy mighty force, from sage and sinner breaks the hymn of glory in thy name. I see the Kuru princes being crushed in battle, with a force so fierce that all the worlds tremble. O Vishnu, tell me, who art Thou?

KRISHNA: O Arjuna, you see me as time that kills, kills those in battle-array who come to die this day, thy cousins who usurped your throne by evil deeds, stand up and fight, vanquish your foes.

ARJUNA: O first among gods, hail to Thee, praise to Thee. I beg Thy forgiveness in addressing Thee as a friend to a friend and called Thee Krishna, not knowing Thy Divine form and hidden majesty. Now I know, for Thou art Father of all below, all above and the worlds within. Now fear mingles with joy, I beg Thee, retake your earthly form of old, as my charioteer in Krishna's form, as my friend and cousin of old.

KRISHNA: O Arjuna, by mystic spell I have

revealed to thee my hidden majesty which no mortal has ever seen before. Now be ready to do battle as your duty.

ARJUNA: O Merciful Lord, I am glad to see Thee in your form of old. Have mercy, Lord!

KRISHNA: Only by fullest service and perfect faith is this privilege granted to those I adore.

ARJUNA: Lord, now I see Thee as my friend that I have known. Forgive my desire to witness Thy form as God.

*With mortal eyes thou cannot behold
the Mystery Supreme in Action.
I give thee Divine Sense and Sight,
now behold my many forms
as Creator and Destroyer.*

Chapter 12
Bhakti Yoga - Religion of Faith

ARJUNA: O Supreme Lord, reveal to me which be the better way of life and faith. To worship and serve Thee as God revealed or as God unrevealed?

KRISHNA: Those who worship and serve me as God revealed are holy and are nearer to God as true devotees. But those who have mastered their sense storms, letting fruits of their labours go as renunciation and worship and serve Me as the One Supreme God are nearer to high heaven. In doing selfless service, these devotees reach me in the end.

Worship in faith, devotion and love of the Lord. With steadfast faith do holy works for God.

O Arjuna, if you fail in this, bring me your

failure, never losing your faith in the love of God. Be honest and truthful with compassion for all, equable in pleasure and pain, hurting none, seeking only good for friend and foe.

With single fervid faith worship the Lord, with full detachment from the material world. Self-realization you will gain, thus Wisdom to obtain.

With single fervid faith worship the Lord,
with full detachment from the material world.
Self-realization you will gain,
thus Wisdom to obtain.

Chapter 13
Separation of Matter from Spirit

ARJUNA: O Keshav, can you reveal to me that which is Matter,
And that which is spirit or Soul and its Nature,
And what is Wisdom and that which is Knowledge?

KRISHNA: This flesh, the body is the field of the self and that which views and knows its activities is the soul. This soul-force or the spirit is guided by God. All the elements of conscious life, the senses, the mind, the unseen vital forces are under the direction of the soul. God guides the spirit in every soul.

The mind, conscious life, senses, the vital life force, all are brought on the matter (body) by the soul. He guides, sustains, surveys and governs the soul. He is the spirit that resides in every soul. He gives wisdom and knowledge, but if the flesh and the spirit between them have strife, let spirit be the guide, wisdom thus to find.

This self-harmony leads to Brahma, the Creator.

Know the Truth that God watches over all nature.
He is the Supreme Spirit in every Soul.
He is the Lord.
He is the Omnipresent God!

He is the Spirit that resides in every Soul.
He gives wisdom and knowledge,
but if the flesh and the spirit
between them have strife,
let Spirit be the guide,
wisdom thus to find.

Chapter 14
Gunatrayavibhaga Yoga

(Religion by Separation from the Qualities)

KRISHNA: This universe is the womb where I plant the seed of all that lives and each mortal is born with these qualities –

> Satwan or soothfastness,
> Rajas or passions,
> Tamas or ignorance.

These qualities bind the Spirit to the flesh. Those with soothfastness are of pure nature. After long austerities, they will reach God. But those of lower nature, where passion and ignorance prevail, pass through rebirths, till their nature becomes pure and soothfast.

ARJUNA: My Lord, what is the nature of those who have mastered passion and ignorance?

KRISHNA: Those who have overcome lust,

passion and ignorance and who worship with single fervent faith, in Oneness with God, the Brahma, will attain and achieve everlasting peace and harmony.

*Those who have overcome lust,
passion and ignorance and
who worship with single fervid faith,
in Oneness with God,
the Brahma, will attain and achieve
everlasting peace and harmony.*

Chapter 15
Religion by Attaining the Supreme

KRISHNA: The aswatha or banyan tree spreads its roots and branches above and below ground, getting nurtured by the sun, the rain and the earth and becomes firmly rooted. Its lesson is like those from Vedas.

Arjuna, cut with an axe of detachment these roots of passion. Be free of delusion and pride and extremes, like pleasure and pain, and find your path to God.

He is the life-giving force in the human soul. He is the Be All and the End All of every Soul.

Arjuna, fix your mind on God in meditation, so shall thou reach God in firmest faith.

By being a true devotee, Arjuna!

Chapter 16
Separation of the Divine from the Secular

KRISHNA: O Arjuna, all beings are marked by their qualities.

Those of godly nature are fearless, charitable. They study and follow the scriptures. They are kind and compassionate.

The ungodly are materialistic. They have insatiable appetites and are hypocritical. They follow lower gods for appearances only.

Some are atheists, ravaged by passion and storms of lust and greed.

The scriptures they do not heed.

O Arjuna, follow the scriptural teaching. When doubts arise, choose to be a truthful being, and take the righteous path to action.

Chapter 17
Threefold Kinds of Faith

ARJUNA: My Lord, those who forsake the scriptures and yet act in full faith, which way do they go at the time of death?

What is their state?
Is it of Satya (truth and purity)?
Or is it of Rajas (passion-ridden)?
Or Tamas (of ignorance)?

KRISHNA: O Arjuna, we are what our faith makes us. By nature we are endowed with fair conscience and at birth have a child's innocence. Of these:
The pure at heart worship one Supreme God.
The passionate ones worship wealth, power and glory.
The ignorant ones live dark and evil lives.
The enlightened souls start their day with Ohm Tat, Sat (prayers) and live in harmony with their Maker, through worship, truth and sacrifice. With full faith they live a holy life.

Concentrating all action to Brahma, they live lives of highest piety.

Those who live lives of pomp and glory, in seeking wealth for personal gain, live lives of passion, of rajas, the ignorant ones live evil lives, harming others for selfish gain, they are of tamas, dark and evil.

Let your gunas be of Satwan, Arjuna. So shall you find salvation.

*The enlightened souls start their day
with Ohm Tat, Sat (prayers)
and live in harmony with their Maker,
through worship, truth and sacrifice.
With full faith they live a holy life.*

Chapter 18
Yoga of Renunciation and Deliverance

ARJUNA: O Lord, by thy favour tell me the difference between Abstention (sanyas) and Renunciation (tyag)?

KRISHNA: Abstention is when you surrender all selfish desires, only doing works of sacrifice, gift-giving and worship. And are in self-harmony, doing your duty, your dharma. Renunciation is the surrender of reward of holy acts. Do all your work unselfishly in worship of the Lord.

Above all, Arjuna, if you have acted in good faith following the scriptures and yet failed, bring me your failure, serve me, true in your faith, love and reverence to Me, so shall thou come to Me.

This I promise, O noble prince, I will free thy

soul from all its sins. Be of good cheer and do your duty. Moksha lies in doing your plain duty. O Arjuna, hide this wisdom from those who have no faith. Teach this knowledge to those who are seekers of Truth. Tell them the true meaning of this, our discourse on the plains of Kurukshetra, following the wisdom of which, none shall perish.

Now have all your doubts vanished, Arjuna?

ARJUNA: By Thy favour I see the light. My doubts are no more. I shall do my duty now according to Thy Word.

SANJAY: This inspiring speech was thus spoken by the Lord of Yoga, enlightening not only Arjuna but all the generations to come.

Teach this knowledge to those
who are seekers of Truth.
Tell them the true meaning of this,
our discourse on the plains of Kurukshetra,
following the wisdom of which,
none shall perish.

Postscript

Prince Arjuna, the disciple, wins the battle at Kurukeshtra. He regains his kingdom, but is saddened by the fact that a whole generation of his family and friends have been slaughtered in the fierce battle. He reigns for many years and is a fair and just king. Towards the end of his life, he seeks out Lord Krishna again and tries to remember his teachings to revitalize the rule of law in his life and in his kingdom.

Gandhiji had this to say about what Gita meant to him:

"...to me the Gita became an infallible guide of conduct. It became my dictionary of daily reference...when doubts haunt me, when disappointments stare me in the face and when I see not one ray of light on the horizon, I turn to the Bhagavad Gita and find a verse to comfort me, and I immediately begin to smile in the midst of overwhelming sorrow."

In the final analysis

Lord Krishna tells Arjuna:

Sarve dharman
Prityajya mam ekam
saranam vraja
Aham tva sarve
papebhyo mokshyami ma suchaha.

The meaning of which is:

Surrendering all activities to me
take refuge in me
I shall free your soul from all its sins
and will take you to eternity.

Saroj Daulat Ram

Ohm

Sarve Dharmanprityaja
Mam Ekam Sharanam Vraja
Aham Tva Sarve Pape Bheyo
Mokshayami Ma Suchaha*

*Surrendering all activities to Me
Take refuge in Me alone
I shall free your soul from sin
and take you to eternity

About the Author

Saroj Daulat Ram was born in Jandiala Guru, India. She lived there as a child before moving to East Africa where she lived until relocating to Dublin, Ireland, to begin her medical studies. After receiving her medical degree, she married S.V. Anand in London, England. She practiced medicine in Nigeria before moving to Nova Scotia, Canada, in 1964. While practicing medicine in Nova Scotia, she founded the India-Canada Association. She moved to Ontario in 1985.

Dr. Ram has three daughters and is an accomplished writer, poet and artist.

www.ingramcontent.com/pod-product-compliance
Lightning Source LLC
Chambersburg PA
CBHW071548080526
44588CB00011B/1828